# DURA·EUROPOS

## THE ANCIENT CITY
## AND
## THE YALE COLLECTION

Susan B. Matheson

YALE UNIVERSITY ART GALLERY

*Fig. 1:* Franz Cumont (left) and Michael I. Rostovtzeff, taken in the Mithraeum after its discovery in 1932.

*Cover:* Heliodoros, the Actuarius. Painted ceiling tile from the House of the Scribes. 3rd cent. A.D. (Yale 1933.292) H. 30.5 cm.

*Frontispiece:* Main Gate, view from the east. (1936–1937)

Copyright © 1982 by the Yale University Art Gallery
All rights reserved
Library of Congress Catalogue Number: 82-50113
ISBN: 0-89467-022-0
Produced under the supervision
of the Yale University Printing Service

The photographs for the cover, Figs. 3, 21, and 30 are by Joseph Szasfai. All remaining photographs are from the Dura-Europos archives in the Yale University Art Gallery.

# FOREWORD

Between 1928 and 1937 Yale University and the French Academy of Inscriptions and Letters conducted excavations at the ancient city of Dura-Europos, situated on the west bank of the Euphrates River in a part of Mesopotamia that now lies within the borders of Syria. Two earlier campaigns had been undertaken by Franz Cumont and the French Academy in 1922 and 1923. Cumont continued to represent the Academy during the joint Yale-French excavations, while the distinguished ancient historian Michael I. Rostovtzeff led the Yale expedition. Maurice Pillet, a French archaeologist, was Field Director for the first four seasons. He was succeeded by Clark Hopkins of Yale in 1932, who served as Field Director through the eighth season. The final two seasons were directed by Frank E. Brown, also of Yale.

As a result of Yale's participation in the excavations and the generosity of the Syrian Antiquities Service, the University received a richly varied collection of close to 100,000 artifacts from the site, representing approximately one half of the finds from the excavations. Most of the remaining objects stayed in Syria and are now kept in the Damascus Museum. This booklet is designed to provide an introduction to the Dura collection at Yale and the city from which it came.

The author would like to thank S. Sidney Kahn, B.A. 1959, whose generous gift has made this publication possible.

# DURA - EUROPOS

## The Ancient City
## and
## The Yale Collection

Dura-Europos was founded around 300 B.C. After the death of Alexander the Great in 323 B.C. the vast empire that he had created dissolved in the struggle for power among his generals and would-be successors. Egypt was controlled by Ptolemy, the founder of the Ptolemaic Dynasty, Antigonos held Macedonia, and by 301 B.C. Seleukos was in firm control of Syria and Mesopotamia.

Numerous cities had been founded in these territories during Alexander's lifetime as part of his policy of Hellenization of conquered lands, and many more were founded by Seleukos and the other Successors after Alexander's death. In the minds of the Successors these new cities were to be strongholds, building blocks in their attempt to consolidate power within their respective territories, as well as vehicles for the dissemination of Hellenic culture. Among these new cities was Dura-Europos.

The precise year of Dura's founding is unknown. Isidoros of Charax, a geographer and historian writing in the 1st century A.D., describes Dura as the "city of Nikanor, founded by Macedonians," but he gives no date. Isidoros was apparently referring to a general of Seleukos named Nikanor, who was governor of the Syrian territory for a time and probably founded a number of military colonies like Dura while holding this position. Nikanor would have founded the city on behalf of Seleukos. The king was regarded as the city's true founder by its citizens, and he was worshipped as such even during Roman times. A limestone cult

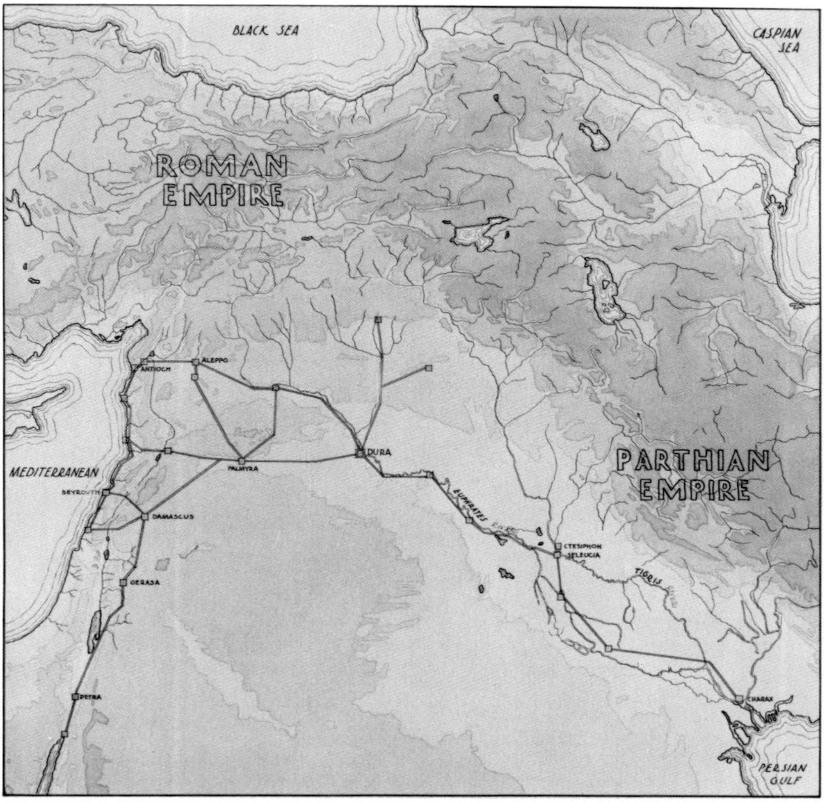
BLACK SEA
CASPIAN SEA
ROMAN EMPIRE
ALEPPO
ANTIOCH
DURA
PALMYRA
MEDITERRANEAN
BEYROUTH
DAMASCUS
GERASA
PETRA
PARTHIAN EMPIRE
EUPHRATES RIVER
CTESIPHON
SELEUCIA
TIGRIS RIVER
CHARAX
PERSIAN GULF

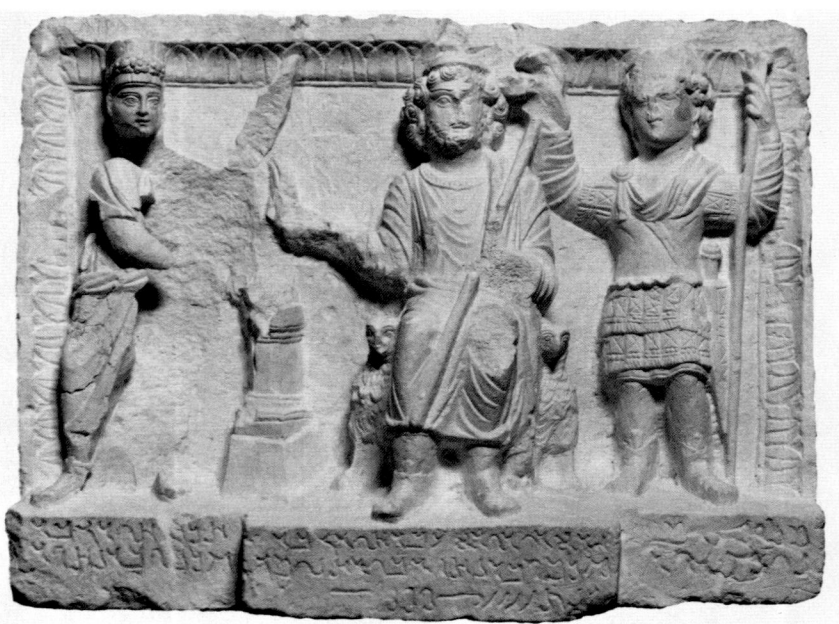

*Fig. 2:* Map of Syria and Mesopotamia, after A.H. Detweiler.

*Fig. 3:* The Tyche of Dura crowned by Seleukos Nikator. Limestone cult relief from the Temple of the Gaddé. A.D. 159. (Yale 1938.5314) H. 62 cm.

relief (Fig. 3) found in the Temple of the Gaddé indicates the prominence of Seleukos in the history of the city. It shows him, identified as Seleukos Nikator in the inscription, wearing military dress and offering a wreath to the *Gad* or *Tyche* (Fortune) of Dura.

The name of the city itself provides further evidence that its founding was connected with Seleukos. Isidoros tells us that the Greeks called the city Europos. The city of Europos in Macedonia was Seleukos' home, and it was common practice in the selection of names for the new Hellenistic cities to commemorate a place with which the founder was closely connected or a member of his family (for example Antioch, the Seleucid capital of Syria, was named after Seleukos' father, Antiochos).

Papyrus documents found at Dura show that its residents called it Europos at least until A.D. 180. The name Dura (or *Doura* in Greek) is Semitic in origin and means "fortress". Documents indicate that the Greek form Doura was adopted soon after A.D. 200, and the name occurs as Dura in a file of Latin letters of the early third century A.D. The compound Dura-Europos is a modern creation.

Europos was founded as a military colony rather than as a self-governing Greek city, or *polis*, although it did achieve this status eventually. The colonists were Macedonian or Greek soldiers, war veterans who were given landholdings in the new city in return for a promise of additional military service when required. These soldiers provided the backbone of the Seleucid army in its wars against the Ptolemies and the Parthians. The military service obligation was permanently tied to the land and was inherited with it by the descendants of the original settlers, as is shown by the copy of a law of succession found in the Dura excavations. The land in a military colony was actually owned by the king, rather than by the city (as was true in a *polis*) or by the veteran and his descendants who cultivated it.

Europos was built on a plateau above the Euphrates River (Figs. 4 & 5). It is bounded on the north and south sides by ravines, and the desert lies to the west. During much of the year the climate was dry, as it is today, and the river provided the main source of water for the settlement and its surrounding farmlands. Because

*Fig. 4:* View of Dura from the air. (1932)

*Fig. 5:* View of Dura from the Euphrates River, showing the citadel. (1936–1937)

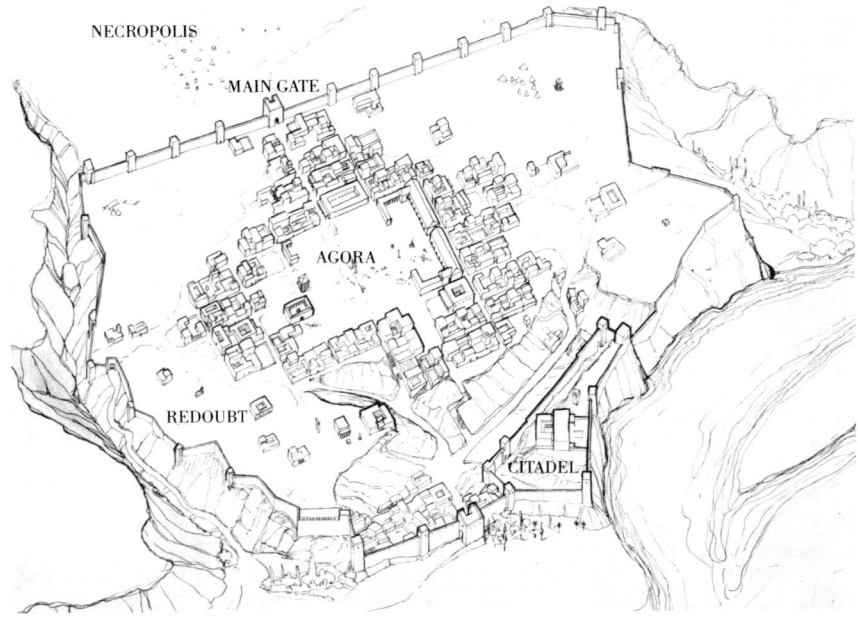

*Fig. 6:* Hellenistic Europos, isometric reconstruction. Drawing by H.F. Pearson.

of the need for irrigation, the land given to the colonists for cultivation extended along the river in both directions from the city.

Europos was laid out on a grid system around a central agora, or marketplace (Fig. 6). This form of city planning is well known in the Hellenistic period, with particularly fine examples surviving at Priene and Miletus in Asia Minor. The city's two main roads intersected at the agora; the east-west road led to the Main Gate on the desert side and to a ravine on the east that led down to another gate at river level. A complete circuit wall with guard towers was built around the city as a defensive measure, another indication of Europos' intended role as a stronghold on a principal route for trade and military campaigns.

Between the ravine leading to the gate on the river side and the river itself an easily defensible piece of high ground was walled in to form a citadel. Remains of a substantial Hellenistic palace were found on the citadel, but it had been ruined by a serious landslide in the 1st century B.C. A smaller and possibly earlier palace, the Redoubt Palace, was found on another outcropping of high ground close to the gate on the river side. This palace may have been used by the city's chief magistrate.

The main part of the city was dominated by the agora, a large square covering an area of eight blocks on the northwestern corner of the intersection of the two main streets. Like agoras in other Greek cities it was open and surrounded by small shops, but it seems to have lacked the long colonnaded buildings (stoas) which defined the perimeters of other agoras of the period. No evidence of a theater, characteristically a part of even the smallest Greek city, was found.

South of the agora, on the other side of the main east-west road, remains of temples dating from the Hellenistic period have been found. These temples apparently stood in a large open space when they were first built, balancing the open space of the agora to the north. The close proximity of the religious and commercial centers of Hellenistic Europos reflects the design of many other Greek cities.

Under Seleucid rule the official religion at Europos was the same as that of other Macedonian colonies in Syria. The leading roles were played by Artemis, Apollo, and Zeus Olympios, the dynastic gods of the Seleucids, and the earliest temple found at Dura was in fact dedicated to Artemis. Although the original dedication of this temple may have been to Artemis and Apollo, after the usual Seleucid custom, the dedication was changed at a relatively early date to Artemis-Nanaia. The fusion of a Greek goddess, Artemis, with a Mesopotamian (primarily Babylonian) fertility goddess, Nanaia, in this dedication represents a phenomenon that was fairly common under Seleucid rule. The population of Europos, like that of most cities in the Seleucid kingdom, was from the beginning a mixture of Macedonian and Greek colonists and local Semitic inhabitants, the latter often the wives and servants of the Macedonians. Seleucid rulers quite willingly tolerated the religious beliefs of the Semitic residents of their cities alongside the official Greek religion, a popular and practical policy which spawned such fused divinities as Artemis-Nanaia and Zeus-Baalshamin and which was ultimately responsible for the survival of the worship of Greek gods in some form throughout the history of Dura. Evidence for other temples built at Europos in the Hellenistic period is scanty.

The remaining buildings in the Hellenistic city were primarily houses, built in the areas surrounding the religious and commercial core. The necropolis (cemetery) was begun outside the city walls, to the west of the Main Gate on the desert side.

Very few artifacts from the Hellenistic period survive. A small number of fragments of imported pottery and glass were found, primarily in the houses. Much of the pottery used at this time seems to have been locally produced commonware. Bronze coins from the reigns of Alexander the Great, Seleukos, Antiochos I, and other Seleucid kings were found. Most of these were from the royal mint at Antioch, but during the reign of Antiochos I a few coins were minted at Europos (280–268 B.C.). This was the only occasion in the city's history when it struck its own coinage. No examples of painting or sculpture from this period have survived, although there undoubtedly must have been some, at least in the temples.

A terra cotta antefix is recorded among the finds, showing that buildings with the characteristic Greek type of tile roof were a feature of the Hellenistic city. Europos was substantially rebuilt in the late 2nd and 1st centuries B.C., and it is otherwise virtually impossible to recover the appearance of the original Hellenistic architecture.

The Seleucid Empire in the 3rd century B.C. spread from Antioch well into central Asia. By the middle of the 3rd century, however, nomadic tribes from central Asia were threatening to invade the eastern borders of the empire. Seleucid control in the east was further weakened by a civil war in the west, which involved hostilities with Egypt and drained men and other resources away from the defense of the eastern provinces. Two of the eastern provincial governors, or satraps, Andragoras of Parthia and Diodotus of Bactria, seized this opportunity to revolt and declare themselves independent. But by 238 B.C. Andragoras had been ejected by the Iranian tribe of the Parni, led by King Arsaces, who thereafter occupied the satrapy of Parthia.

Arsaces' conquest of Parthia was but the first step in the formation of the empire of the Parni, or the Parthians as they were soon to be called. For the remainder of the 3rd and most of the 2nd century B.C. the Parthians battled the Seleucids for control of the territory from Bactria to the Euphrates River. By 141 B.C. the Parthians had captured Babylon, and they moved up the Euphrates to take Dura-Europos around 113 B.C. The city seems to have surrendered without a struggle.

The Parthian kings were relatively liberal in the amount of autonomy they permitted their provincial governors and the cities of their empire. The Seleucid territorial divisions were retained at first, although the smaller subdivisions of the old satrapies evolved into primary administrative units by the 1st century B.C. Greek cities and military colonies, such as Dura, which had been "free" under Seleucid rule were allowed to retain their constitutions and laws.

Greek was adopted by the Parthian rulers as their official language and used for their coins and official correspondence. Aramaic, a Semitic language, was widely spoken in the western Parthian Empire. Bilingual inscriptions in Aramaic and Greek found at Dura show that both languages were in use there. The Parthian language itself occurs more rarely than either Greek or Aramaic, and at Dura it was used for graffiti and other casual inscriptions rather than official documents.

A multitude of religions coexisted under the tolerant Parthian rule. Greek and Semitic divinities and beliefs were often fused in the cults of western Parthia as they had been at Dura under the Seleucids. Babylonian, Aramaic, Arabic, and Phoenician gods were worshipped, along with purely local divinities who produced fertility, good crops, and rainfall, and were often shown armed as protectors of their devotees.

Many of these cults existed at Dura, and under Parthian rule the city enjoyed a prosperity sufficient to encourage the building of new temples and the remodelling of old ones. Temples to the Semitic gods Bel, Iarhibol, Atargatis and Hadad, and Aphlad were built between 50 B.C. and A.D. 50. The largest temple at Dura, that of the Graeco-Semitic fertility goddess Artemis-Nanaia, was rebuilt between 40 and 32 B.C. Temples to Zeus Kyrios–Baalshamin and Zeus Theos were dedicated in A.D. 29 and A.D. 114 respectively. In a final flurry of Semitic piety a new Temple of Bel and a Temple of the Gaddé (Fortunes) were built, the latter finished just prior to A.D. 159.

The new temples were oriental in plan and appearance, in contrast to the Seleucid temples which seem, from the scanty evidence surviving, to have had plans in the Greek tradition with Doric columns and open courtyards for the altars. The original Temple of Artemis had a plan of this kind, but when it was rebuilt after a fire in the mid-1st century B.C. the open courtyard was replaced by a walled sanctuary complex with a major shrine *(naos)* opposite the only entrance and subsidiary shrines lining the interior sanctuary wall (Fig. 7). This type of plan was used for eight other temples built at Dura in the Parthian period, and it determined the general appearance of religious architecture for the remainder of the city's history.

The interior decoration of these Parthian temples also diverged from that of

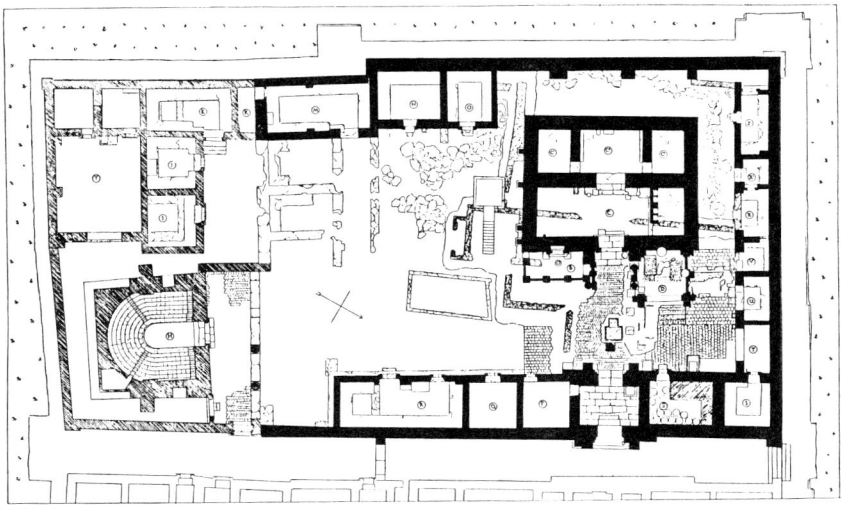

*Fig. 7:* Temple of Artemis-Nanaia, plan. The dark section shows the Parthian plan; the light section represents the Roman expansion. Plan by A.H. Detweiler.

*Fig. 8:* Temple of Zeus Theos, naos, cult painting. 2nd cent. A.D. Reconstruction drawing by F.E. Brown.

their Greek predecessors of the Seleucid era. Even in temples whose dedications were purely Greek, such as the Temple of Zeus Theos, a large wall painting of the deity replaced the traditionally Greek sculpted image (Fig. 8). The paintings were Iranian in appearance and iconography. Zeus Theos was shown armed and in Persian dress, standing in front of a chariot which charged toward the right edge of the picture. The frontal poses of all the figures and the discrepancy in scale between the god and his associates are basic characteristics of Iranian style. Indeed, the only Greek touch remaining in this cult image is the pair of flying Nikes (Victories) crowning the god. Scenes of devotees offering sacrifices to the deity were arranged in registers on the side walls of the shrines. Occasionally these scenes were represented in relief sculpture rather than painting (Figs. 9 & 10).

Some cult reliefs showing images of the deities were discovered in temples at Dura (Fig. 11), but most were found in the subsidiary shrines and thus were not the primary cult images. Like the reliefs showing scenes of sacrifice, these reliefs are often similar in style to paintings. An oriental fascination with linear patterns of drapery and details of costume, rather than the Greek emphasis on the relation of drapery to anatomy, characterizes the sculpture and painting of Dura. Stasis

*Fig. 9:* Zeus Kyrios-Baalshamin (seated) and dedicant. Limestone cult relief from the Temple of Zeus Kyrios. A.D. 31. (Yale 1935.45) H. 52 cm.

*Fig. 10:* Aphlad (right) and dedicant. Limestone cult relief from the Temple of Aphlad. A.D. 54. (Damascus Museum) H. ca. 51 cm.

*Fig. 11:* Atargatis (right) and Hadad. Limestone cult relief from the Temple of Atargatis. 2nd cent. A.D. (Yale 1930.319) H. 41 cm.

*Fig. 12:* Aphrodite standing on a tortoise. Marble. 2nd cent. B.C. (Louvre) H. 56 cm.

replaces movement, and stiff frontal figures are preferred to the Hellenistic Greek style that survived in a few imported sculptures (Fig. 12).

The two centuries of peace that followed the Parthian conquest of Dura were the most prosperous years in the city's history. Her position on the trade routes connecting the Persian Gulf and Seleucia-on-the-Tigris with Palmyra, Antioch, and the Mediterranean Sea brought camel caravans to the city and with them wealth to the local merchants. The open Greek marketplace in the center of the city was transformed into a crowded oriental bazaar. Elaborately decorated houses, as well as the temples described above, were built with these new private fortunes. Although superficially like Hellenistic Greek houses at Priene and elsewhere in the arrangement of their rooms around a central courtyard, the Dura houses diverged from the Greek plan in their use of irregularly shaped rooms and an angled entrance to the central courtyard (Fig. 13). Their decoration consisted of cast plaster cornices and painted walls, but the painting was limited to washes and bands of solid colors.

Dura was also a political center of some importance under Parthian rule. The provincial governor administered his territory from Dura. Sometime around the middle of the 1st century B.C., as noted above, a large portion of the cliff which formed the citadel fell into the river, taking about half the Citadel Palace with it. As a result, the citadel was abandoned, and it appears that from then on the Parthian governor lived in the Redoubt Palace instead. No administrative buildings were built under the Parthians, but a few commercial buildings in the agora area were converted into government offices.

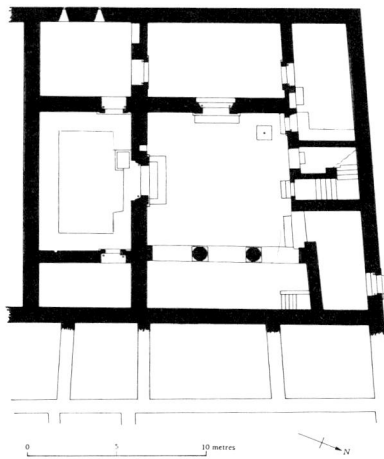

*Fig. 13:* Typical house plan, Parthian period. Block M8, subsequently the Christian Building.

*Fig. 14:* A Parthian cavalry soldier (*clibanarius*). Both he and his horse wear metal scale armor. Graffito from a private house, subsequently the Christian Building.

Parthian control of the Tigris-Euphrates valley was first challenged by Rome in the mid-1st century B.C. Crassus, who along with Julius Caesar and Pompey the Great formed a triumvirate which ruled Rome from 59–54 B.C., launched an unprovoked and unpopular campaign against Parthia in 55 B.C. He crossed the Euphrates on the attack in the spring of 53 and almost immediately encountered a formidable Parthian army. The Battle of Carrhae, on 6 May 53 B.C., was a disaster for the Romans. They succumbed completely to the heavily mailed Parthian cavalry (Fig. 14), and by the end of the three day contest Crassus was dead and thirty thousand Roman soldiers had been killed or taken prisoner by the Parthians. The Roman military standards, the famous Roman eagles, were also in the hands of the Parthians.

By their victory the Parthians had proven their power and established the Euphrates as their western frontier. An abortive invasion across the river by Marc Antony in 33 B.C. failed to change this situation, and in 20 B.C. the new emperor, Augustus, made peace with Phraates IV, the Parthian king. The Roman standards and many of the prisoners from the campaigns of Crassus and Marc Antony were returned to Rome. The terms of the peace treaty established the border between the two empires on the Euphrates at its junction with the Khabur River, forty miles upstream from Dura. Dura remained under Parthian rule.

The Parthians maintained the borders of their empire intact until the Roman emperor Trajan began his eastern campaigns in A.D. 113. After annexing the kingdoms of Armenia and northern Mesopotamia as Roman provinces, Trajan turned eastward toward Seleucia and the Parthian capital, Ctesiphon. In A.D. 116, Dura was captured, and Trajan erected a triumphal arch commemorating the event on the desert road to the west of the city. He may have left a garrison to hold the city, but if so it was only there for a short time. After Trajan's death in A.D. 117, the new emperor, Hadrian, restored the old frontiers. The Euphrates-Khabur junction once again marked the Parthian border, and Dura was once again under Parthian rule.

The Roman army returned to Dura in A.D. 165, under the command of the emperor Lucius Verus on another eastern campaign. The Parthians were expelled from the city and a garrison was installed. Verus made Dura a permanent frontier post on the new eastern border of the Roman Empire. This time the Romans had come to stay. Dura became a Roman colony under the emperor Caracalla (A.D. 211–217), and it remained Roman until its final destruction in A.D. 256.

The Roman occupation brought significant changes in the appearance of the city (Figs. 15 & 16) and the lives of its inhabitants. In some cases these changes were not for the better. In spite of the military importance that Dura enjoyed, the standard of living of the civilians in the city seems on the whole to have been lower than it had been under Parthian rule.

The most basic and obvious change was one that confronts all cities which must host a military garrison, the designation of part of the city as living quarters for the soldiers. The first Roman garrison at Dura was small, but when it was enlarged under Caracalla in the early 3rd century, the northwest section of the city was walled off to form the Roman camp. Many of the houses in this residential

*Fig. 15:* Roman Dura, plan. Drawn by David O. Kiphuth.

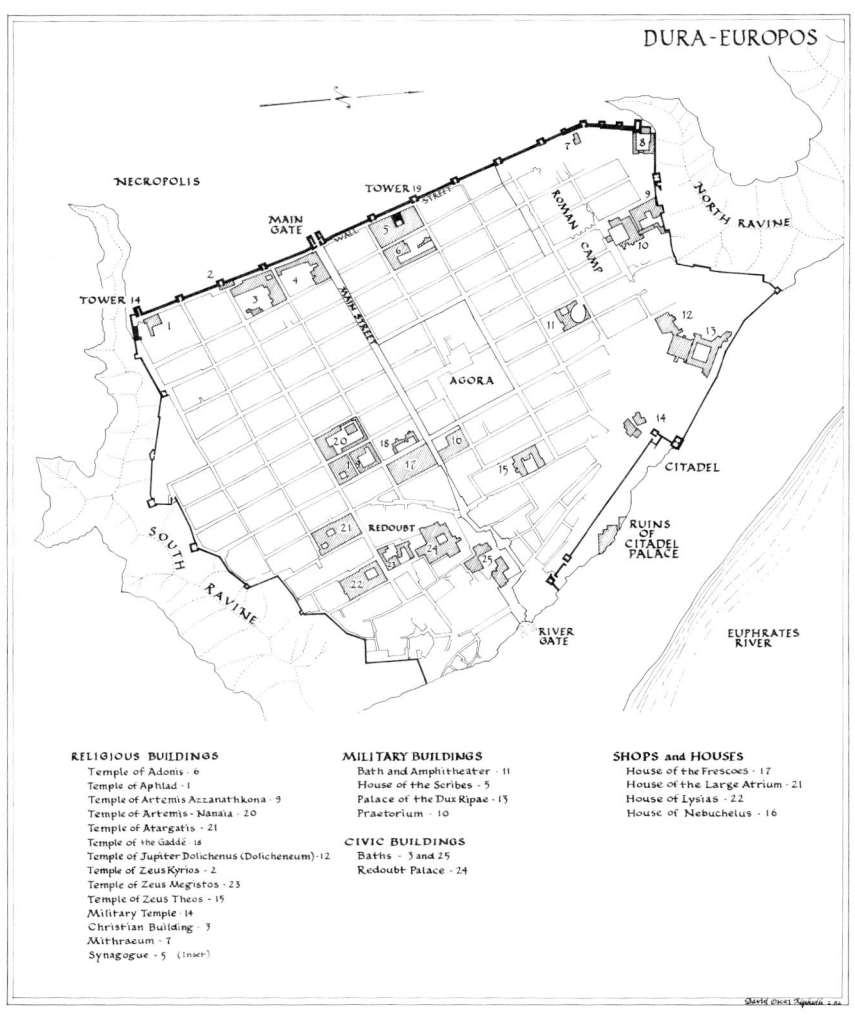

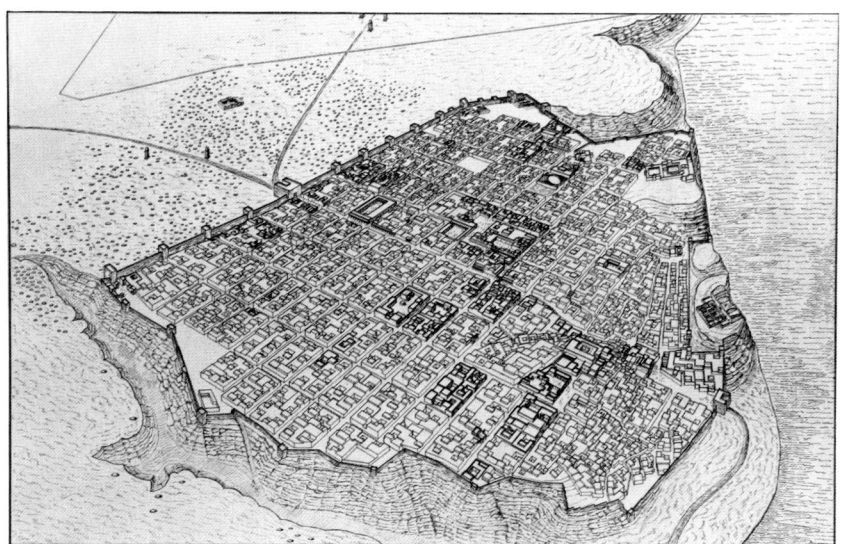

*Fig. 16:* Roman Dura, isometric reconstruction.
Drawn by N.C. Andrews.

district were razed to the ground to make room for the characteristic features of a Roman camp: the *praetorium* (headquarters), officers' houses, a bath, and the *campus martius*, where military drills and parades were held. Other houses were converted into barracks.

Only two temples which predate the Roman occupation were left standing in this section after the urban renovation, the Temple of Azzanathkona and the Temple of Bel. On the eastern side of the camp a large new temple was built and dedicated to Jupiter Dolichenus, an oriental god popular among the Syrians who made up most of the legions stationed at Dura and the surrounding areas. A small shrine to Mithras was dedicated by a group of Palmyrene archers in A.D. 168–170/71, shortly after the Roman occupation began. The shrine was rebuilt with considerable elaboration after the enlargement of the garrison in A.D. 209–211, and a third time around A.D. 240 (Fig. 17).

Shrines to Mithras, called *Mithraea*, have been found throughout the Roman Empire. Originally an Iranian god, Mithras became especially popular among Roman soldiers and the merchant class. His cult was a mystery religion that featured initiation, a ritual banquet, and the promise of salvation after death. Only men were allowed to join. Mithraic shrines were generally underground, commemorating the god's birth in a cave. The Dura Mithraeum is unusual in that it was totally above ground.

*Fig. 17:* Mithraeum, final phase. Ca. A.D. 240. Excavation photo, *in situ*, 1932.

The devotional focus of a Mithraic shrine was typically a cult relief showing Mithras slaying the Cosmic Bull, symbolizing the victory of light over primaeval darkness. Two such reliefs were installed in the Dura Mithraeum (Fig. 18). Their inscriptions show that they date from the earliest phase of the shrine, but they continued to serve as the cult images in subsequent renovations. Both reliefs show Mithras and the Bull in characteristic fashion: Mithras, dressed in Persian costume, sits on the back of the Bull and pulls his head back with one hand while he stabs the animal in the neck with the other. A small dog drinks the blood from the wound. In the larger of the Dura reliefs the donors or dedicants of the relief are shown to the right of this scene, another diversion from normal Mithraic iconography for which the Dura Mithraeum is notable.

Surrounding the two reliefs are series of paintings showing scenes from the life of Mithras, signs of the zodiac, and, once again, Mithras slaying the Bull, this time in a landscape with trees and altars. To the left and right of the reliefs appear two seated single figures of prophets or magi, who, like Mithras, wear Persian dress. On the side walls of the niche are two virtually identical scenes of Mithras as a mounted archer hunting wild animals in a wood (Fig. 19). These hunting

*Fig. 18:* Mithras slaying the Cosmic Bull. Limestone cult relief from the Mithraeum. A.D. 170/71. (Yale 1935.98) H. 76 cm.

*Fig. 19:* Mithras as a mounted hunter. Wall painting from the Mithraeum. ca. A.D. 240. Excavation photo, *in situ*, 1932. (Yale 1935.100) H. ca. 1.70 m.

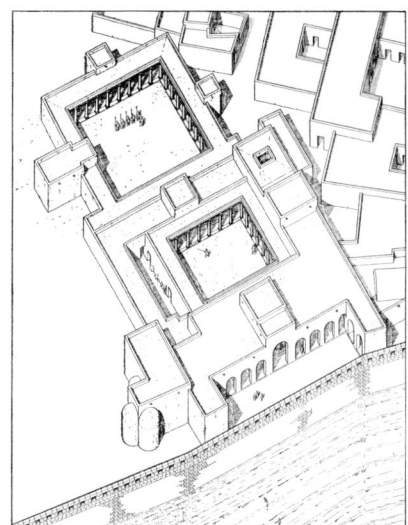

*Fig. 20:* Palace of the *Dux Ripae*. 3rd cent. A.D. Isometric reconstruction drawing by A.H. Detweiler.

*Fig. 21:* The tribune Julius Terentius sacrificing to the gods. Wall painting from the Temple of Bel. Ca. A.D. 239. (Yale 1931.386) H. 1.07 m.

scenes are particularly Iranian in character and unparalleled in Mithraea in the western Roman Empire. The paintings described here and preserved in the reconstructed shrine at Yale are from the last redecoration of the Dura Mithraeum, which took place around A.D. 240. Fragments surviving from the renovation of ca. A.D. 210 indicate that it had similar paintings.

The last major building erected at Dura was the palace built in the 3rd century for the Roman commander of the River Bank (Palace of the *Dux Ripae*). The *Dux* was the officer in charge of the defense of the west bank of the Euphrates River, the empire's eastern frontier. He does not appear to have played a significant role in the daily administration of the Dura garrison. The palace was situated in the northeast corner of the city, overlooking the river. It was Roman in style, with two large peristyle courtyards surrounded by public and private rooms (Fig. 20).

Much has been learned about the composition and administration of the Dura garrison from the written documents and inscriptions found in the excavations. The early garrison included the Palmyrene archers, who may have been at Dura before the Roman occupation, and the Ulpian cavalry, which took part in Lucius Verus' Parthian campaign. After the garrison was increased in the 3rd century, the largest unit was the Twentieth Palmyrene Cohort (*Cohors XX Palmyrenorum*). This unit is known only from the papyri and inscriptions at Dura, where it seems to have had its headquarters.

One of the unit's commanders, Julius Terentius, dedicated a wall painting around A.D. 239 in the Temple of Bel on behalf of his soldiers (Fig. 21). The painting shows a sacrifice to the gods, who appear as statues of armed deities in the upper left. The commander, who is identified by the inscription, offers the sacrifice on the altar in the center. He is flanked by his soldiers and the unit's standard. The Tyches (Fortunes) of Dura and Palmyra appear seated in the lower left. Like the Palmyrene gods to whom the temple is dedicated, the Tyches were protectors of the people.

More than 200 written documents on parchment and papyrus from the files of the XXth Palmyrene Cohort were found in the excavations. Among these documents are rosters of the men in the unit, lists of officers, letters from Provincial Headquarters assigning mounts to the cavalry, daily reports on the strength and activities of the unit, and a calendar of the official Roman festivals which the soldiers were required to observe. The papyri tell very little of the campaigns and other events in which the XXth Palmyrene participated, but they do give a picture of an ordered daily existence that was similar to that of many Roman outposts.

Smaller detachments from other Roman legions were brought to Dura from time to time to strengthen the garrison. Although they were less permanent residents than the XXth Palmyrene Cohort, these soldiers nevertheless took part in the building and improvement of the military camp. Members of two Syrian legions rebuilt the Mithraeum in A.D. 209–211 and contributed to the rebuilding of the Temple of Jupiter Dolichenus in A.D. 211. A few years later, in A.D. 216, two similar detachments erected an amphitheater.

Less drastic changes occurred in the appearance of the civilian section of the city, although some Romanization was evident here as well. Two new baths were constructed, one near the Main Gate and the other off Main Street near the Redoubt. Main Street was given colonnades near the agora.

Far more significant were the increasingly crowded conditions under which the civilian population lived. Residents displaced by the Roman military camp joined other residents and newcomers in subdivided houses elsewhere in the city. In most Roman cities the increasing population settled in suburbs outside the city walls, but at Dura the existence of the necropolis outside the west wall of the city prevented expansion of the residential area in the only direction the terrain permitted. The need for safety also encouraged the people to live inside the walls.

The civil administration was probably still in the Redoubt Palace, and the chief magistrate may also have lived there as he seems to have done in the Parthian period. The old Temple of Artemis was expanded in the 3rd century, with part of the new section serving as the senate chamber.

Some of the largest and most elegant houses were concentrated around the Redoubt, with a few others elsewhere in the city. Many were rebuilt or redecorated in the Roman period. These houses testify to the fact that at Dura, like Atlanta during the American Civil War, some people made a good profit supplying goods and services to the soldiers. Traces of painted walls and molded plaster cornices show that these houses were quite Roman in appearance, despite the fact that their owners often had Iranian names. One of these houses, outside the military camp, was taken over to provide quarters for army officials. This building, the House of the Scribes, has yielded one of the most captivating paintings from Dura, a portrait of Heliodoros the Actuarius, or keeper of military records (see cover).

The demographic character of Dura's civilian population probably did not change much in the Parthian and Roman periods. The distant descendants of the original Macedonian settlers, if any still survived, had long ago intermarried with local residents, and the population as a whole seems to have been primarily Semitic and Iranian. Many of the soldiers, although Roman legionaries, were in units raised locally and were thus also of Semitic or Syrian origin.

Latin was the official language of the Roman military, but civil documents at Dura were still written in Greek. Laws of succession and inheritance were still based on Hellenistic Greek prototypes. Taxes were collected by the civil administration. Marriage was by contract, with a property settlement, and divorce was permitted. Records of loans, deeds of sale, and other contracts were kept in a Registry Office. The documents found in this office during the excavations have contributed significantly to our ability to envision life at Dura. Aramaic continued to be used in graffiti, and knowledge of Hebrew among the Jewish residents can be demonstrated from a written copy of a Hebrew prayer used after meals.

A small Jewish community was well established at Dura by the late 2nd century A.D. A house near the western city wall was converted into a synagogue sometime between A.D. 165 and 200. Although simple at first, the synagogue was enlarged and elaborately redecorated around A.D. 244/245. Paintings of Old Testament subjects covered the walls of the assembly hall, and the ceiling was filled with painted tiles (Fig. 22).

*Fig. 22:* Synagogue, view of the NW corner showing the Torah shrine. Ca. A.D. 240. (Reconstructed in the Damascus Museum)

Like other synagogues, the Dura synagogue was oriented west, toward Jerusalem. The Torah shrine was in the center of the west wall. Surrounding it were scenes of the finding of Moses, Samuel anointing David, the Exodus (Fig. 23), and the Temple of Jerusalem, among others, while above it were King David and the generations of Israel. The vision of Ezekiel appeared on the north wall, and the rest of that wall, along with the south and east walls, bore other biblical scenes.

The style of these pictures is typical of most of the paintings at Dura, and of the sculpture as well. There is little in it that is reminiscent of Greek art, in contrast to cities like Antioch where the Greek artistic tradition remained strong. Dura's paintings have been called the "oriental forerunners of Byzantine painting," and their preference for frontal poses, schematic rendering of the human figure, and loving attention to decorative detail and linear pattern at the expense of naturalistic proportions, anatomical veracity, and movement can indeed be described as oriental traits.

The presence of figural paintings in the Dura synagogue apparently ignores or contradicts the biblical second commandment, which prohibits "graven images," and is certainly unusual if not unparalleled in early synagogues. Elaborate cycles of wall paintings are quite characteristic of other religious buildings at Dura, however, and their use in the synagogue could be explained as conformity to local custom. The members of the Dura congregation may have been making a distinction between "graven images," statues or cult images that were regarded as

Fig. 23: The Exodus. Wall painting from the Synagogue. Ca. A.D. 240. (Damascus Museum) H. ca. 1.16 m., L. 4.66 m.

embodiments of the deity and actually worshipped, and paintings which conveyed messages of Jewish unity and redemption. Whatever its reasoning, the Jewish community at Dura was exceptionally liberal in its attitude toward the scriptural injunction against images.

The same prohibition played an important role in the development of early Christian art and generated widespread controversy among theologians of the early Church. Most of our knowledge of Christian art in the first three or four hundred years after Christ is based on the catacombs in Rome. The paintings which decorate these catacombs show that Christian art in this period was primarily symbolic. Old Testament subjects which were recognized as symbolic of the deliverance or salvation promised by Christ, such as Jonah and the whale and Daniel in the lion's den, occur frequently, while representations of the Crucifixion, the Last Supper, and the narrative cycles of the life of Christ so common in mediaeval art are notably absent. The figure of Christ appears only in symbolic form, as the Good Shepherd, another reference to the promise of salvation. Miracles of Christ which could be linked to this theme, such as the healing of the paralytic, were also represented. Some of the leaders of the early Church believed that even this symbolic type of art violated the prohibition of the second commandment, and they were particularly adamant in their desire to keep Christian places of worship free from pictorial decoration of any sort.

The first Christian congregations worshipped in private houses, meeting to celebrate the Eucharist at the homes of their wealthier members on a rotating basis. By the 2nd century A.D. there is evidence that some of these houses were donated to the congregations and converted into churches. Just such a conversion took place at Dura around A.D. 240.

Since Christian worship was still proscribed and subject to persecution in the 2nd and 3rd centuries, it was necessary for Christian places of worship to be discreet, if not completely secret. Thus the converted house-church usually, as at Dura, showed no change on the exterior. Worship was generally conducted in the atrium, or central courtyard, of the house. Here the early church at Dura differs, in that the meeting hall used for worship and prayer was created by knocking down the wall between two adjacent rooms off the left side of the atrium (Fig. 24). Across the atrium, on the right side, another room was transformed into a baptistery, richly decorated with Christian paintings. Clearly Dura's Christian congregation, like its Jewish community, did not adhere strictly to the prohibition against images.

*Fig. 24:* Christian Building. Ca. A.D. 240. Plan. (cf. Fig. 13)

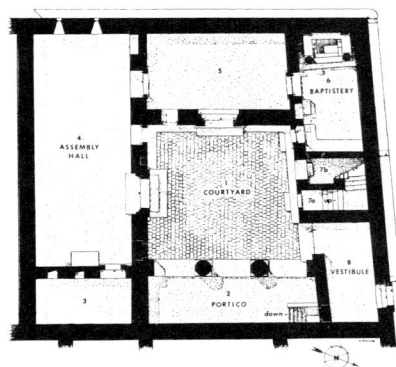

The Dura baptistery was a small room with a baptismal font under a columned vault at one end (Figs. 25 & 25A). Baptism was by immersion at this time, and the font was large enough to hold a person. A painting of Christ as the Good Shepherd appeared on the wall above the font. The remaining three walls bore subjects from the New Testament: the Samaritan woman at the well, Christ walking on the water,

*Fig. 25:* Christian baptistery. Ca. A.D. 240. Excavation photo, *in situ*, 1932.

*Fig. 25A:* Christian baptistery, model.

Christ healing the paralytic (Figs. 26 & 26A), and the women visiting Christ's tomb after the Resurrection. One Old Testament subject, David and Goliath, was also represented, and there are traces of a scene suggesting Paradise. A small drawing of Adam and Eve was added to the Good Shepherd fresco at some point after its completion.

Baptism and the Eucharist were the two most important sacraments to the early Christian Church. Both were viewed as signs of the salvation promised by Christ to his followers. The subjects chosen for the Dura baptistery paintings were thus particularly appropriate because they all symbolize in some way the idea of deliverance or salvation. In this respect the Dura paintings are comparable to the paintings in the Roman catacombs and also serve as evidence that prototypes for thematic cycles of mosaics showing Christ's miracles and their Old Testament counterparts existed in the early Church. The controversy over the use of pictorial decoration in the Church was ultimately resolved in its favor. In the words of Pope Gregory the Great (ca. A.D. 600), "Pictures are used in the church so that those who are illiterate may by looking at the walls read there what they are unable to read in books."

*Fig. 26:* Christ healing the paralytic. Wall painting from the Christian baptistery. Ca. A.D. 240. Excavation photo, *in situ*, 1932. H. 1.46 m.

*Fig. 26A:* Christ healing the paralytic. Drawing by H.F. Pearson.

One of the most remarkable things about Dura in the Roman period is the variety of religions that were practiced there. The old Greek gods of the Seleucid era still played a prominent part in the religious life of the city. The protector god of Dura, its Tyche or Gad, was still Zeus Olympios, the patron god of Seleukos and Alexander the Great. He appears, as we have seen, crowned by Seleukos, the deified founder of Dura, in a cult relief of the 2nd century A.D. (Fig. 3). The relief was dedicated by Palmyrene inhabitants of Dura in the Temple of the Gaddé, along with a companion relief of the Tyche of Palmyra. Among the other Greek gods worshipped at Dura in this period, Herakles, Artemis, and Aphrodite were especially popular. As before, they were frequently worshipped jointly with their oriental counterparts.

The majority of gods worshipped at Dura under Roman rule were Semitic, consistent with the city's religious history. Atargatis and Hadad, Bel, Iarhibol, and Aphlad were still of primary importance, and their temples continued to receive dedications of paintings and reliefs. Some of these new dedications were encouraged by the rebuilding necessary after an earthquake in A.D. 160. The Temples of Artemis-Nanaia and Zeus Megistos, among others, show evidence of renovation at this time. The fusion of Greek and Semitic deities which characterized the earlier religious history of Dura certainly persisted until the end.

The particular contribution of the Romans to Dura's religious environment was the introduction of the official Roman pantheon, the gods and goddesses of Rome and the deified members of the imperial family. The calendar of official Roman holidays found in the military camp shows that the soldiers at Dura were subject to the same religious requirements as soldiers elsewhere in the empire. In addition, however, the Dura soldiers, many of whom were recruited locally, favored certain oriental gods such as Mithras, Jupiter Dolichenus, and Iarhibol, as we have seen from the shrines and other dedications to those gods in the Roman camp. Judaism and Christianity were the other newcomers to Roman Dura, but these were religions of the civilian rather than the military population.

*Fig. 27:* Necropolis, reconstruction showing the tower tombs. Drawing by H.F. Pearson and N. Toll.

The eclectic nature of religious life at Dura is also reflected in the necropolis. The tombs there were of two types. The most striking undoubtedly were the huge tower tombs, which had niches or *loculi* around the outside of the base for mummified bodies (Fig. 27). Similar tower tombs were found at Palmyra, but there the burial niches were on the inside, and each was sealed with a portrait bust carved in relief. There were no such reliefs at Dura. The second type of tomb was the underground chamber, a type found throughout the Syro-Palestinian area, with burial *loculi* carved out of its stone walls. Although chamber tombs or catacombs of this kind were used by Jews and Christians elsewhere in this period, there were no tombs at Dura which could be proven to have served followers of either of these religions.

More than forty of the chamber tombs were excavated, along with a rubbish heap that seems to have resulted from the clearing up after the earthquake of A.D. 160. Many of the tombs had been looted, some in Antiquity and others after the rediscovery of the site in 1920, but a group of undisturbed tombs under the Roman dump heap yielded pottery, figurines, lamps, and jewelry which could be closely dated and formed a sequence useful in dating objects from elsewhere in the city.

These small finds and the thousands more that were found in the houses,

*Fig. 28:* Head of a young woman named Baribonnaea. Wall painting from the Temple of Zeus Theos, naos, side wall, 2nd register. 2nd cent. A.D. (Yale 1935.93) H. ca. 47 cm.

*Fig. 29:* Green glazed amphora. 1st-early 2nd cent. A.D. (Yale 1938.4843) H. 32.5 cm.

shops, barracks, and streets add a richness of detail to our picture of life at Dura. From them we have learned that residents of Dura wore garments of wool and cotton, some of which had colored borders, used cut pile rugs similar to our Orientals, employed a variety of elaborately decorated textiles in their houses and public buildings, and appreciated the rarity and quality of silk imported from China. Some wore leather shoes, with stamped or embroidered decoration. Others wore straw sandals. Jewelry was worn by both men and women, and while most of it was bronze, some splendid silver bracelets, gold earrings, and gold and silver necklaces were found. Wall paintings in the temples fill out the picture suggested by these finds (Figs. 28 & 8) and show that Dura's citizens were fashionable in an Eastern rather than a Greek or Roman style, like the men and women shown in Palmyrene funerary reliefs.

Household utensils consisted largely of pottery vessels, which were used for cooking, storage, shipping, and eating. Affluent families used imported Greek and Roman pottery for eating and storing toilet articles. Locally made commonware was used for cooking by these households and served all functions for the lower classes. During the Parthian period an attractive green glazed ware was introduced (Fig. 29), a type of pottery that occurs wherever the Parthians ruled. Numerous

*Fig. 30:* Silver vase with gilded Bacchic frieze. 3rd cent. A.D. (Yale 1931.585) H. 22 cm.

fragmentary glass vessels were found, including drinking cups, plates, and perfume containers. Glass was also used for windows. A few examples of wood and bone boxes and powder containers were found, and a small group of baskets has also survived. Fishhooks, tweezers, needles, and similar small utensils were generally made of bronze, as were scalpel handles and other medical instruments.

Very few of these household objects could be described as luxurious. Exceptions include the silk mentioned above and a large silver vessel with a gilded frieze of Bacchic motifs (Fig. 30). Objects imported from farther away than Palmyra have not turned up in large numbers. Despite Dura's position on a major trade route, her population depended heavily on local products throughout the city's history. The archaeological evidence suggests a community whose residents generally never had more than a moderate income, with a few affluent families and a larger number whose income was well below average. By the middle of the 3rd century A.D. the city's economic life had shrunk to the point where even the most prosperous businessmen conducted their money-lending and retail trade only locally and on a very small scale. Dura's relative prosperity had been destroyed by the coming of Rome.

Rome, of course, was not particularly concerned. Other developments demanded her attention. One of the major reasons for maintaining a Roman garrison at Dura, and the primary reason for strengthening it in the 3rd century, was the rise of the Sasanian Empire to the east. The Sasanian kings had succeeded the Parthian dynasty as rulers of Iran. Taking advantage of challenges to Roman power on other frontiers, the Sasanian king Shapur I launched an invasion of Syria in A.D. 256. The Roman emperor Valerian took the field in person against Shapur, but after a disastrous defeat at Edessa in A.D. 258 Valerian was forced to sue for peace. The Sasanians had marched up the Euphrates River to take Antioch, the Syrian capital, and captured everything along their route, including Dura.

This time Dura did not surrender without a struggle. Defensive embankments of gravel and debris were constructed along both the inside and outside of the western city wall. The larger embankment on the inside of the wall filled the buildings along Wall Street, preserving, incidentally, the paintings in the synagogue, the Christian baptistery, and the Mithraeum under the rubble. The embankments were designed both to counteract direct attacks by troops and battering rams and to keep the wall from collapsing and forming a breach if a mine were dug underneath it (Fig. 31). In fact they succeeded only in part.

The Sasanians were deterred from a direct frontal attack, but during a siege of

the city they undermined two guard towers (Tower 19, two blocks north of the Main Gate, and Tower 14, in the southwest corner of the city's defensive wall) and built an assault ramp near Tower 14. A third mine was dug near the ramp and a fourth was constructed directly beneath it. It appears that these mines originated inside the city, suggesting that they were countermines dug by the Roman defenders. Another countermine was dug against the mine under Tower 19. All the mine tunnels were supported by timbers. Once the mines were completed it was an easy task to set fire to the timbers, causing the collapse of the tunnels and the structures above them.

The final attack can be dated by a remarkable find in the mine tunnel under Tower 19. Skeletons of soldiers who were caught in the collapse and died in the tunnel still retained handfuls of Roman coins, none of which dated from later than A.D. 256. These coins provide firm evidence that the fall of Dura occurred as part of Shapur's invasion of Syria in A.D. 256–258. An impressive amount of military equipment was found with the skeletons, including chain mail shirts, an iron helmet, shields, and arrows. Much of this armor is more Persian than Roman in appearance, which has led some to suggest that the soldiers were attackers rather than defenders, in spite of the fact that they were carrying Roman coins. The question is complicated further by the possibility that there was fighting in the tunnel before it was burned, leaving wounded soldiers to die in the collapse.

*Fig. 31:* Fortification wall. Note that the embankment only shows in the distance; the foreground embankment has been removed by the excavators. (1936–1937)

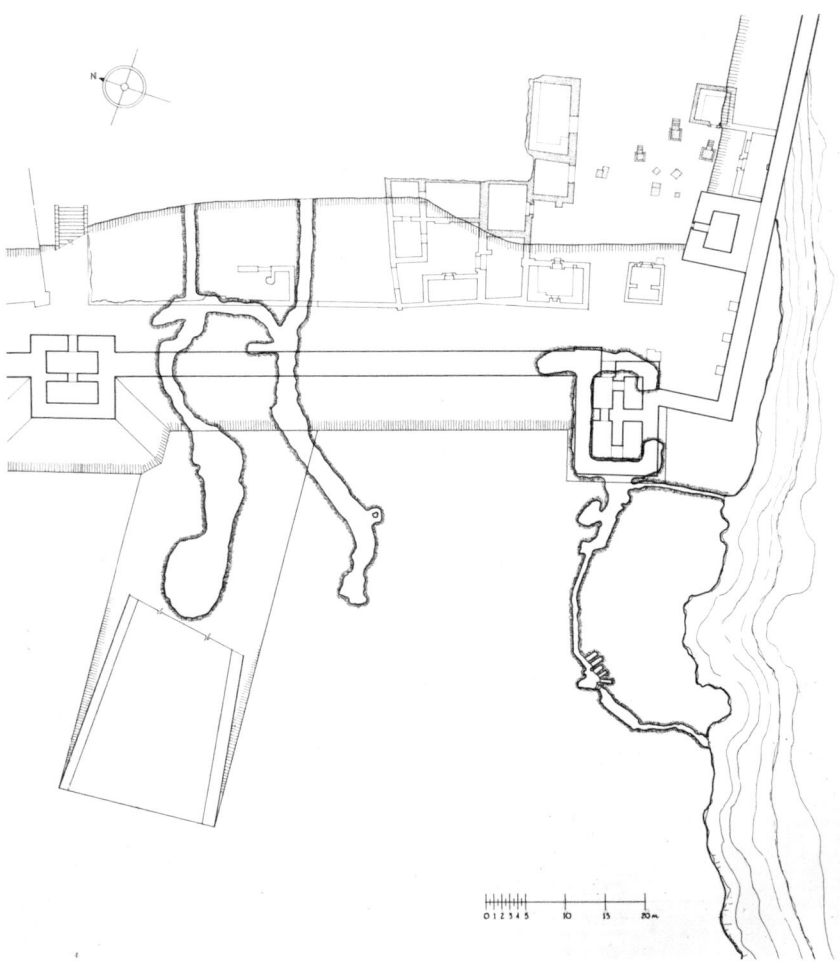

*Fig. 32:* Map showing the Sasanian mine under Tower 14 (right) and the countermines under the Sasanian assault ramp. The Tower 14 mine begins in the south ravine and traverses two tombs before reaching the tower. Drawn by N. C. Andrews.

Fig. 33: Konon sacrificing to the gods. Wall painting from the Temple of Bel. 2nd cent. A.D. (Damascus Museum) The discovery of this painting by British soldiers in 1920 was the first event in the series which led to the excavation of Dura.

Once its defenses were breached the city must have surrendered, since there is no evidence of fighting in the town or any indication that the Sasanians burned the city. After the Persian victory the inhabitants must have been driven out, perhaps carried off and sold into slavery, for there is no record of settlement at Dura from this time onward.

Dura remained abandoned to the desert until it was rediscovered by British soldiers in 1920 (Fig. 33). The first archaeologist to examine the

*Fig. 34:* Main Gate, view from inside the city. (1936–1937)

ruins was an American, James Henry Breasted, who explored it only for a day shortly after its discovery. It was Breasted who identified the city as Dura, from the inscription on the Terentius fresco (Fig. 20) uncovered by British soldiers. Its identity was confirmed by the first inscription found by the Yale expedition, on the city's Main Gate:

ΕΥΧΑΡΙΣΤΩ ΤΗ ΤΥΧΗ ΔΟΥΡΑ — "I thank the fortune of Dura"

# SUGGESTED READING

*General References on the Site*

Rostovtzeff, M.I. *Dura-Europos and its Art*. Oxford, 1938.

Perkins, Ann. *The Art of Dura-Europos*. Oxford, 1973.

Hopkins, Clark. *The Discovery of Dura-Europos*. Ed. Bernard Goldman. New Haven, 1979. With an excellent bibliography.

*Excavation Reports*

Cumont, Franz. *Fouilles de Doura-Europos*. Paris, 1926. 2 vols.

Baur, P.V.C., and M.I. Rostovtzeff, et al., eds. *The Excavations at Dura-Europos. Preliminary Reports of the First-Ninth Seasons of Work, 1928–1936*. New Haven, 1929–1952. 8 vols. in 10 parts.

*The Excavations at Dura-Europos. Final Reports*. New Haven, 1945–1969 and Los Angeles, 1977. 5 vols. in 11 parts, including vols. on sculpture, pottery, textiles, lamps, bronze objects, glass, parchments and papyri, coins, the synagogue, and the Christian building.

Cumont, Franz. "The Dura Mithraeum," trans. and ed. by E.D. Francis, in *Mithraic Studies* I. Ed. J.R. Hinnells. Manchester, 1975.

*General Historical References*

Tarn, W.W. *Hellenistic Civilization*. 3rd rev. ed. New York, 1974.

Colledge, M.A.R. *The Parthians*. London, 1967.

Cary, M. *A History of Rome down to the Reign of Constantine*. 2nd ed. London, 1965.